CHATHAM
AND
GILLINGHAM
IN OLD PHOTOGRAPHS

CHATHAM AS YOU HAVE NEVER SEEN IT! A rare view of HMS Pembroke naval barracks showing a scene from the September 1913 pageant in which members of the public were invited to see a spectacular play entitled *In the Far East*. Taking place on the parade ground, it involved 400 men who took various parts in the play. Money collected was donated to the Royal Naval and Marine Orphan Home in Gillingham. Further pictures of the production can be found on pages 144–145.

CHATHAM
AND
GILLINGHAM
IN OLD PHOTOGRAPHS

COLLECTED BY
PHILIP MACDOUGALL

ALAN SUTTON
1989

Alan Sutton Publishing
Gloucester

First published 1985

British Library Cataloguing in Publication Data

Chatham and Gillingham in old photographs.
1. Kent, history
I. MacDougall, Philip
942.2'3

ISBN 0-86299-682-1

Typesetting and origination by
Alan Sutton Publishing
Printed in Great Britain by
Dotesios Printers Limited

CONTENTS

ainham from the Air, looking North

A VIEW OF RAINHAM VILLAGE as seen from the church tower during the 1930s. Station Road is seen with the premises of W. & R. Fletcher (butcher's of No. 1 Station Road) clearly visible. On the nearside of this shop is a former school, while on the opposite side of the road are the premises of the Rainham & District Co-operative Society. This can be best placed by reference to the horse-drawn delivery van which is standing in their yard. Further views of this area of Rainham can be found on pages 48–52. (Graham Smith.)

INTRODUCTION

This book is primarily a collection of photographs showing the towns of Chatham and Gillingham during earlier years. In addition, consideration is given to the adjoining communities of Luton, Brompton and Rainham. Although once completely separate they have, over the years, become closely integrated into the wider townships of Chatham and Gillingham. For this reason, the entire area can be usefully treated as a single entity. First, however, a brief reference to how each of these communities changed from being independent tiny villages to the huge combined conurbation that they currently represent.

Undoubtedly, the most important single factor in the development of virtually the entire Chatham and Gillingham area was that of the naval dockyard. Established around the year 1570, the dockyard had an immediate effect on Chatham. Sited in close proximity to the parish church of St Mary's, it was natural for those initial groups of artisans and labourers employed in the yard to find accommodation within the neighbouring village of Chatham. Over the following years, as the dockyard expanded, so did the community of Chatham. From a mid-sixteenth century population of around 250 Chatham had, by the mid-seventeenth century, acquired a population that was ten times that number. Effectively, therefore, Chatham could no longer be considered a village but was, instead, one of the largest towns in Kent.

For Gillingham, the pace of growth was much slower. With the centre of the parish over a mile from the dockyard, few of those early dockyard artisans chose to live in the original village. Some, however, began to acquire houses in a part of Gillingham parish that was known as Brompton, an area lying even closer to an enlarged seventeenth-century dockyard than the rapidly expanding central part of Chatham town. Expansion of Brompton was eventually limited by the Chatham and Gillingham Lines, with Brompton appearing to reach its maximum point of growth around the mid-eighteenth century.

Luton was the next community to witness a period of expansion that was brought on by the dockyard. Lying to the south-east of Chatham town, housing had been creeping towards Luton throughout most of the earlier years of the yard's existence. Eventually, as the demand for land became increasingly desperate, dockyard artisans began to take up residence within the village of Luton, a move that eventually led to a continuous band of housing which now inextricably links the two communities of Chatham and Luton.

It was a massive extension to the dockyard, undertaken during the reign of Queen Victoria, that led directly to the creation of present day Gillingham. This extension, which brought the boundaries of the dockyard into the parish of Gillingham, resulted in a local housing boom in a previously undeveloped part of the parish. This was the area of Gillingham in the vicinity of the present day High Street which, at that time, was known as New Brompton. On this land, hundreds of small terraced houses were built. The growth of New Brompton is easily traceable by minute changes in housing design and conveniently placed date stones with which many of these houses were completed. Eventually, to avoid confusion, the entire area adopted the name Gillingham.

Of the various communities examined in this book, only Rainham was to be more-or-less unaffected by the growth of the dockyard during these years. Having a relatively small population at the beginning of the nineteenth century, it did witness a period of marked expansion in later years. This was partly the result of the establishment of a brickworks, usefully sited to supply the needs of builders working upon the construction of houses in Chatham and Gillingham. For its later expansion, Rainham has tended to attract commuters, with most of its housing dating to a more recent period.

This, then, is the background to the development of the Chatham and Gillingham area. The illustrations in this book date primarily from the late Victorian and Edwardian periods. By that point in time, the Gillingham extension to the dockyard was in full operation. Chatham had a continuous belt of housing that ran from its western boundary with Rochester right through to the village of Luton. Gillingham, which was still known as New Brompton at that stage, was developing at an extremely rapid pace. Housing had crept on to the south side of the High Street, a point which was further away from the dockyard, with a number of new estates having either been completed or still under construction.

To help travellers reach the dockyard, and other points in Chatham, Gillingham and Rainham, the start of the new century coincided with work constructing a tramway system that would eventually serve the entire area. Appropriately, therefore, it is an imaginary journey on part of this completed system that provides the opening section for the book.

Hold very tight please as we begin a journey into the past . . ..

SECTION ONE

A Journey into
the Past

*Darland Banks – Luton – The Brook – Military Road – Dock Road – Old
Brompton – High Street, Gillingham – Railway Street, Chatham – Town Hall,
Chatham – Watling Street – London Road, Rainham*

*In June 1902 the Chatham and District Light Railway Company brought a
transport revolution to the Medway towns. In that month it began taking
fare-paying passengers on its newly completed tram routes that had been
established throughout much of Chatham and Gillingham. Before that date,
local travellers had either to walk to their destination or make use of a limited
number of horse-drawn cabs or buses. This opening section of the book
attempts to relive the days of the tram by taking the reader on an imaginary
journey from Luton to Gillingham before looking at one or two other routes.*

BEFORE JOINING OUR TRAM for that imaginery journey, it might be an idea to take a closer look at the tram depot which stood on the south side of Luton Road. Imagine it is around 1910 and that we are standing at the top of Darland Banks. Below can be seen the rapidly expanding village of Luton (sometimes known as Cabbage Island). On the right, and easily recognizable by its tall dark chimney, is the tram depot. This is our first stop before catching a tram from outside the Hen and Chickens (often shortened to Hen and Chicks) in Luton High Street. (Kent County Library Photo.)

APPROACHING THE DEPOT, its layout soon becomes a little clearer. Consisting of a power-station, offices and two linked car sheds, it was an essential component for the entire system. Within the sheds, which are to be seen to the left of the main complex, a total of 60 trams could be parked at any one time. Those needing maintenance could be taken into an expansive workshop area while the sheds were also fitted with a number of special pits. Before entering the depot it is worth taking a more general look at Luton. To the left of the depot a number of hay-ricks can be seen. Clearly, during the early years of the century, Luton was still a semi-rural community, although the majority of its inhabitants were employed in the dockyard. (Les Collins.)

HAVING REACHED OUR FIRST PORT OF CALL, it would seem natural to walk around the depot and take a closer look at the power-station. Completed in 1902, this station supplied all the electric power needed to keep Chatham and Gillingham trams running. Within this rather inelegant building were located a series of boilers and compound engines originally supplied by Yates and Thom of Blackburn. Today, the depot site is owned by Maidstone and District and is used to accommodate buses. However, only the sheds of this original depot have been retained. (Mr C. Taylor.)

WITHIN THE DEPOT MAINTENANCE AREA we catch our first glimpse of a tram. Resplendent in a green and ivory livery, the name of the company (Chatham and District Light Railway) can be seen emblazoned in gold-shaded lettering upon the rocker panel. This particular tram was one of an initial batch of 25 which was supplied to the Chatham company just before it began operating its first routes in 1902. With the body of the tram built by the Shropshire firm of George F. Milnes, it had seating for 24 on the lower deck and room for a further 28 on the upper deck. The driver, as can be noted from this picture, had little protection from the elements. (Mr C. Taylor.)

HAVING SPENT A FEW INTERESTING MOMENTS in examining the tram depot it is time to step on board one of those noisy clanking machines that were once such a familiar sight throughout much of the Medway area. Outside the Hen and Chickens, which served as the Luton terminus, a near empty tram is already waiting. Unlike the car already seen with its maintenance crew at the depot, this is one of a batch that was delivered in 1907. Built at Loughborough by the Brush Electrical Engineering Company it was a slightly smaller vehicle with a seating capacity of 48. Clearly a carefully posed photograph, this was also taken around the year 1910. (Les Collins.)

AFTER LEAVING THE TERMINUS, this Gillingham-bound tram moves along Luton Road (the subject of this photograph) before entering the intersection of several routes at Luton Arches. This picture gives some idea of the work involved in setting up the tramway system, with heavy metal rails sunk into the roadway and numerous traction poles having to be erected. In all, the route between Luton and Gillingham took nearly two years to complete. (Les Collins.)

IT IS ALSO IN LUTON ROAD that we catch a glimpse of the depot works car. Used for maintenance work throughout much of the system, it was actually built in the Luton depot, the truck and electrical equipment having been salvaged from a tram involved in a serious crash at Brompton on 30 October 1902. (Les Collins.)

AFTER PASSING ALONG PART OF CHATHAM HIGH STREET our tram from Luton approaches the Town Hall via the Brook. Because all of Medway's tram routes converged upon the Town Hall, it is likely that a number of fellow passengers will alight at this point, joining trams heading for Rochester or Rainham. As for our Gillingham-bound tram, this will pass in front of the Town Hall before continuing along Dock Road.

IT WAS THE DOCKYARD WORKER who probably benefitted most from the new tram system. Providing a cheap and regular means of urban transit, hundreds of labourers and artisans no longer had to waste 30 or 40 minutes in a daily trek from the more distant parts of Luton and Gillingham. Frequent trams stopped at the Main Gate (seen here at the turn of the century) with a further service running the full length of Dock Road before terminating outside Pembroke Gate.

THE ROUTE TO GILLINGHAM passed the dockyard's Main Gate before turning right and entering Old Brompton (via Middle Street). At one time trams had used the more steeply inclined Westcourt Street, but this part of the system had been abandoned following a crash in which a tram had gone down hill too fast. It was the car which was damaged in this crash which had been subsequently converted into the works car seen in Luton Road. In this photograph one of the trams supplied by the Milnes company is seen entering Westcourt Street on its journey back to Chatham.

AFTER TRAVELLING ALONG BROMPTON ROAD our tram eventually reaches Gillingham High Street where it catches up with another of the Milnes-supplied trams, this one having just completed the journey from Frindsbury.

High Street, Gillingham.

AS THE TRAM CONTINUES along the High Street it passes over a trackway junction which allowed trams to enter the High Street from Canterbury Street. These trams would also have come from Chatham, travelling via Watling Street. Again, this photograph was taken around 1910, with the little altered Prince Albert pub to be seen on the right.

A VIEW ALONG CANTERBURY STREET showing a tram heading back towards Chatham. Like most of the trams running throughout the Medway towns, this one carries a variety of advertisements, including one for the Chatham Intra store of Featherstone's. Taken around 1919, this photograph shows a 'Maidstone and District' bus timetable for petrol-driven buses. These served the more distant routes that were beyond the tramway system. (Kent County Library.)

AFTER A FEW MORE MINUTES, our tram eventually stops outside Gillingham station. This is not the present day station, but an earlier one that was built further along Railway Street. Leaving the tram at this point allows us to catch a train back to Chatham. (Graham Smith.)

THE STATION FORECOURT at Chatham as seen around the turn of the century.

HAVING ARRIVED BACK AT CHATHAM, a short walk along Railway Street will bring us to the Town Hall. On the way it is worth taking a look at the New Road viaduct. This was completely rebuilt in 1902 in order to ensure that trams could pass beneath it. The cost of its reconstruction was jointly borne by the tram company and Chatham council.

CONTINUING ON FOOT to the Town Hall we come across another tram, this one having New Brompton on its indicator board. New Brompton was the former name for the central part of Gillingham, the whole area being re-designated Gillingham from 1903 onwards. However, trams continued to show New Brompton on their indicator boards for a good many years after the official name change.

A GENERAL VIEW OF RAILWAY STREET as seen from the New Road viaduct. Although this picture was taken over 80 years ago, there are remarkably few changes to those buildings closest to where the photographer was standing. Further back, however, both the Pentagon and a new road layout have brought a number of severe alterations to this part of Chatham.

Chatham, Military Road.

THIS PICTURE, taken in 1905, is a very different Military Road to that of today. A number of older Victorian shops have since been replaced by Mountbatten House and the entire road system has changed. As we return to the Town Hall it would be difficult not to notice the large numbers of soldiers and sailors who emanate from the various local barracks. The tram heading in our direction is bound for Chatham Cemetery and may well have soldiers on board who will alight at the old Southhill Barracks (now a depot for council vehicles).

ARRIVING AT THE TOWN HALL we have a choice of several trams. In fact, throughout most of the day, trams would be passing every five or six minutes. This time, taking a tram to Rainham, we will return along the Brook before heading up Chatham Hill. Prior to leaving Chatham a glance towards the Town Hall will show how little this building has changed. Completed in January 1900 it currently serves as an arts centre.

HAVING ASCENDED CHATHAM HILL, Rainham-bound trams would pass over the junction with Canterbury Street. Here, some trams turn left to enter Gillingham. Those that continued towards Rainham might eventually reach a speed of 16 mph, as there was a special section alongside the road for the sole use of trams.

FOR RAINHAM a particularly memorable event was the arrival of its first tram in August 1906. Here, for the purpose of celebrating the event, a crowd has gathered outside the Cricketers Inn. (Kent County Library.)

THE LAST TRAM TO OPERATE IN THE MEDWAY TOWNS ran on Tuesday 30 September 1930. Travelling on a route that took it from the Royal Naval barracks to Rainham Road, the event was marked by crowds of spectators who lined much of the route. Chatham Town Hall proved a particular focal point, many of the onlookers rushing to board the vehicle. Some of those unable to clamber on board simply followed behind. With the event completed by the singing of 'Auld Lang Syne' it must, indeed, have been a very sad event. On the following day all of the tram routes were being operated by Leyland Titan buses belonging to the old tram company which had now become the Chatham and District Traction Company. This photograph is of the tram graveyard that was established alongside Watling Street on that special piece of roadway that had been reserved only for the running of trams. Over the following months they were sold off to anyone who could afford them. (Les Collins.)

The Church Supreme

*St Margaret – St Mary – St Barnabas – St John – St Michael the Archangel –
Bible Christian Chapel, Luton – Christ Church – Salem Chapel – Garrison
Chapel – Jezreel's Tower*

*During the Middle Ages the church was very much at the centre of the
community. Within the parishes of Chatham, Gillingham and Rainham large
sums of money were frequently spent on improving the three separate church
buildings, the emphasis often on their general enlargement. Despite this, the
three original parish churches were quite unable to serve the needs of an area
that, throughout the nineteenth century, was undergoing a process of rapid
expansion. The result was that a number of additional churches were built,
designed to serve those who lived further afield or who did not subscribe to the
established faith.*

St. Margaret's Church, Rainham,

THE PARISH CHURCH at Rainham as it appeared towards the beginning of the present century. A solid ragstone building that boasts the usual mixture of architectural styles so common in English parish churches. The original building is thirteenth-century but evidence of numerous later additions abound. Supposedly haunted, it is said that a headless nobleman makes a frequent nocturnal visit before he is driven away by a carriage drawn by headless horses and driven by a headless coachman. Personally, I have my doubts!

A VIEW OF THE PARISH CHURCH at Rainham as drawn in 1813. (Kent County Library.)

AT GILLINGHAM, St Mary the Virgin was the original parish church around which the early village first clustered. The later influence of the dockyard created the much larger township of New Brompton, leading to the construction of a series of newer churches such as that of St Mark's in Canterbury Street.

THE LARGE BUILDING which can be seen towards the centre of this general view of Nelson Road is the Church of St Barnabas. One of several Victorian churches in the area, it was designed to fulfil the needs of the newly increased population of Upper Gillingham. St Barnabas was designed by J.E.K. and J.P. Cutts and completed in the year 1890. Despite the fact that this photograph was taken during the reign of King Edward VII, the road has changed remarkably little, with only one or two new houses to be seen.

THE INTERIOR OF CHATHAM'S ST JOHN'S CHURCH as seen in a 1905 postcard view. As it happens, this was one of several postcards sold by the church to augment its funds. The church was constructed in the Classical style and completed in 1821 at a cost of £14,157.

ANOTHER NINETEENTH-CENTURY CHATHAM CHURCH that drew upon an earlier age for its chosen architectural style is that of St Michael the Archangel. Located in Hills Terrace, it was completed in 1863 and still serves the local Roman Catholic community.

AN INTERIOR VIEW of the Bible Christian Chapel that once stood in Luton Road at the junction with Connaught Street. Completed in 1885 it was later acquired by the Methodists. (Les Collins.)

A FURTHER VIEW of the Luton Road Bible Christian Chapel in its days as a Methodist church. Built in red brick with decorative turrets and a rose window looking out on to the Luton Road, it cost a mere £1,800 to build. Eventually demolished in the 1980s it also came to the rescue of the local Anglican community when it temporarily replaced Christ Church during the time in which that church was being rebuilt. (Les Collins.)

LUTON has seen the construction of three separate buildings that have adopted the name Christ Church. All built within close proximity to one another, the earliest of these is the brick building seen to the left in this photograph. Built in 1843 it was designed by Inwood and George. (Les Collins.)

THE SECOND CHRIST CHURCH at Luton was constructed in 1884 and took over the role of that earlier church. As a result, the first Christ Church at Luton was converted into a church hall. Both buildings survived into the twentieth century, with the earlier Christ Church eventually demolished in the 1970s. The second Christ Church was replaced by the present Christ Church built in the mid-1980s. (Les Collins.)

A BUSY SCENE outside Luton's second Christ Church. Almost certainly the final moments of an Armistice Day service, a former vicar, the Revd Phelps, can be seen on the extreme left. The lych-gate still survives. Originally it stood alongside Luton Road, but it has since been removed to the Upper Luton Road side of the new church. (Les Collins.)

SALEM CHAPEL, LUTON. Once situated in Crittenden's Meadow (now the Luton recreation ground) it became, in later years, a changing room for local football teams. (Les Collins.)

AMONG CHURCHES IN THE AREA which had mainly military congregations was the Garrison Chapel which was built in the 1840s at a cost of £10,000. Still in use, it stands at the top of Maxwell Road.

UNDOUTEDLY one of the best known religious buildings in the area was Jezreel's tower. Demolished in 1961 it was an obvious landmark that was clearly visible for many miles. Standing close to Watling Street, the sight of this building must have raised many unanswered questions from passing motorists who were on their way to Margate or one of the other Kent coastal resorts. In this picture the famous building has been borrowed by the Chatham Motor Company to advertise a new range of coaches. (Chatham Motor Company.)

Jezreels Tower, Gillingham, Kent 074

A MORE FAMILIAR VIEW of the famous tower, built by an obscure religious sect during the latter part of the nineteenth century. Never completed, for the Jezreelites ran out of money, it was designed as a headquarters building that would have contained offices, stores, a library and an assembly room.

SECTION THREE

The High Street Trader

Chatham Intra – Chatham High Street – Gillingham High Street – Skinner Street – Luton High Street – Naval Barracks – Station Road – Rainham High Street.

Shopping, during the twentieth century, has undergone a revolution which has seen the virtual demise of the independent high street retailer. As a result, most of the nation's shopping centres lack any real character, each of them offering a similar round of shops dominated by companies such as Tesco, British Home Stores and W.H. Smith. In this section, which centres upon shops and shopping during the early part of the present century, emphasis is placed upon the large number of locally based retailers that once controlled the High Street scene.

Featherstone's Outing, Boulogne-sur-mer, 7th July 1914

FEATHERSTONE'S, once situated in the Chatham Intra section of the High Street (but having a Rochester address), must be considered as the most prestigious of the area's early shops. Among various departments were those specializing in fashion, house furnishings, cycling and the sale of coal. This particular photograph, taken in July 1914, portrays members of Featherstone's club during an outing to Boulogne. With over 1,000 members of the club going to France on that occasion, it had been necessary to book three special trains to convey all of them out of the Medway towns so that they might catch the steamer *Empress* from one of the Channel ports. Apparently, the event proved a great success, with the entire eight hours abroad being spent in unbroken sunshine. Sad to relate, this was the last Featherstone's club outing prior to the declaration of war in August. Of the 1,000 club members who joined the party on that day, a number of them must have been recalled to France under very different circumstances.

HIGH STREET, CHATHAM.

CHATHAM HIGH STREET in 1938 as seen looking towards the junction with Military Road. Burton's (centre right) has only just left this particular site, while the Lloyd's building has been considerably modernized. In the distance shops belonging to the locally based outfitters of F. & H. Newcomb (No. 133 High Street) and Style & Mantle (No. 117 High Street) are recognizable from the advertisements placed on the side of their respective premises.

High Street, Chatham showing the Empire.

SHOPS IN THE VICINITY of the now demolished Empire Theatre as seen shortly before the outbreak of the First World War. The Empire itself specialized in the staging of music hall acts (see page 85) and had a seating capacity of 2,500. As for the shops in this particular area of Chatham High Street, there is a varied collection that includes Nunn's clothing and hosiery store (far right) and the cash price chemist's owned by H. Cook & Co. (extreme left).

AN EARLIER VIEW of the same section of Chatham High Street as previously described. The Empire Theatre is again visible, although partly obscured by a number of Union Jacks. Of special note is the large variety of delivery trucks which are mostly horse-drawn. During a busy part of the day these could create a traffic jam every bit as severe as those found in the present day High Street.

GILLINGHAM HIGH STREET, c. 1910. Compare this photograph with the one reproduced on page 18. Both are part of the same series, although this one provides a clearer view of the Prince Albert pub. Surprisingly, the pub has undergone remarkably few changes – even the window boxes appear to be in exactly the same position! Immediately next door to the Prince Albert is another of the numerous locally based outfitters that were once to be found throughout Chatham and Gillingham. On this occasion it is Edwards and Gittings (Nos. 76 & 78).

THE FORMER POST OFFICE at Gillingham as it appeared during the years before the First World War. Situated in Skinner Street it had only the status of a branch office placed under Rochester and Chatham. Although no longer a post office, the building continues as Omar's Steak and Kebab House.

SHOP STAFF employed in the Gillingham branch of Marks and Spencer. Probably photographed during the 1920s, they are seen standing outside the original Marks and Spencer bazaar (No. 145 High Street). It was in 1933 that the present shop (No. 151–3) was opened. (Marks & Spencer plc.)

AS A MEMORIAL to Winston Churchill upon his death in 1965 many local shops displayed wreathed pictures of the former Prime Minister. This one appeared in the Gillingham branch of Marks and Spencer. (Marks & Spencer plc.)

A LOCAL DELIVERY CART collecting or delivering items to one of Gillingham's High Street shops around 1910.

THE FIRST GARAGE to be built at Luton (and on the site of the present day garage). Converted from a number of old cottages the pumps are selling Power Petrol, a commodity that used to be produced on the Isle of Grain.

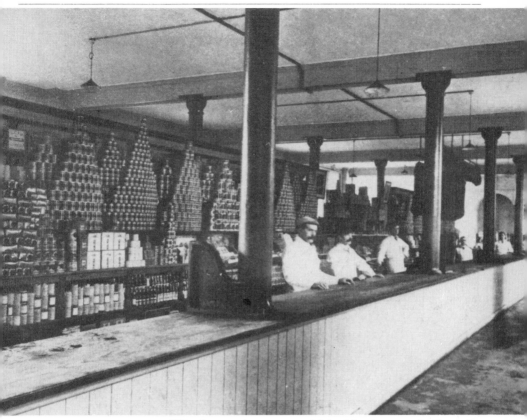

WITHIN THE NAVAL BARRACKS at Gillingham a shop was established for the use of ratings. As can be seen from this picture, it was well stocked with various canned products.

ALTHOUGH A RATHER GRUESOME PICTURE it does demonstrate how meat was once commonly sold. Instead of the homogeneous packaging used by the modern-day supermarket, customers got very definite proof of what they were buying. The shop depicted belongs to Alfred Callaway and was once situated at No. 3 Station Road, Rainham. Callaway, who described himself as a pork butcher, is to be seen at the front of his shop. (Kent County Library.)

STATION ROAD, C. 1927. Rainham, at that time, was a relatively small community and had none of the national chains that were then beginning to creep on to the High Streets of Chatham and Gillingham. Alfred Callaway's shop is to be seen on the left, immediately next door to the premises of W.R. Fletcher (also a butcher's shop). The railings belong to the local school while the newsagent's shop (on the far side of Callaway's) was owned by Fred Kitney. (Graham Smith.)

STATION ROAD looking back to the point from which the previous two photographs were taken. Again, Alfred Callaway's shop is visible (to the right) and a full view of the school is also included. On the left, the side of the premises belonging to the Rainham & District Co-operative Society are visible, with their advertisement indicating the range of goods sold. (Graham Smith.)

A MORE DETAILED VIEW of shops owned by the Rainham & District Co-op. This picture was taken a few years prior to the First World War and shows that the store has been prepared for the forthcoming sales bonanza otherwise known as Christmas. (Kent County Library.)

PART OF RAINHAM HIGH STREET as viewed looking east. The first shop on the left is that of Charles Kitchingham, a butcher, while other shops in this group include a cycle agency, a stationer's and a greengrocer's. (Graham Smith.)

MANY OF THE SHOPS in the previous picture are to be seen in this slightly earlier view of Rainham High Street. The most obvious point from which to take bearings is the rather tall telegraph pole which is to be seen in both photographs. Rainham Post Office stands on the left. (Kent County Library.)

RAINHAM HIGH STREET looking back to the point from which the previous two photographs were taken. (Kent County Library.)

A FINAL VIEW of Rainham High Street as seen during the 1950s. (Graham Smith.)

SECTION FOUR

The Working Day

The royal dockyard – Luton waterworks – Luton hop farms – Gillingham and Chatham schools – Gillingham Road – Darland Banks.

This section looks at various aspects of the working day, concentrating on paid employment within the towns of Chatham and Gillingham. It begins with a study of the dockyard. This was once the largest employer in the Medway area with a workforce in excess of 8,000 even before the turn of the century. Consideration is also given to a more reluctant group of individuals who were partly responsible for constructing a massive extension to the dockyard built during the latter part of the nineteenth century. Finally, attention is given to other aspects of working life in Chatham and Gillingham.

A SUPERB VIEW of the ship fitters' shop as it appeared around 1902. Constructed during the nineteenth century, the shop specialized in the production of materials to be used in vessels recently built or repaired within the yard. As can be seen, it was a massive building and employed a large number of skilled and semi-skilled workers. During the nineteenth and early-twentieth centuries, the dockyard took increasing numbers of workers, encouraging people to move into the Medway towns from areas as far afield as Scotland, Wales and the West Country.

THE DOCKYARD TORPEDO FITTING SHOP. Again employing a number of highly skilled artisans, the torpedo shop was located close to the No. 3 basin. It was constructed towards the end of the nineteenth century, at a time when torpedoes were first being developed as a weapon of war.

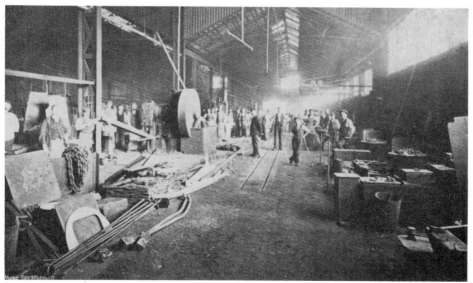

THE DOCKYARD SMITHERY. Possibly one of the least desirable of the yard work areas, as those employed here had to put up with the heat of numerous fires. It was in the smithery that anchors and various other iron items were manufactured through the process of heating iron bars and then beating them into shape with the assistance of mechanical hammers.

A CRUISER IN DRY DOCK. In this photograph members of the dockyard workforce are employed upon the hull. The dockyard at Chatham was responsible for both the building and repair of warships together with the fitting and refitting of these ships before they joined the fleet.

PAY-DAY AT THE DOCKYARD. In return for their wages, labourers and artisans at the yard had to work from 7 a.m. until 5 p.m. during summer time and 7.30 a.m. until 4.00 p.m. during winter time with additional hours worked on Saturday morning.

LABOURERS AND ARTISANS are seen leaving the yard's main gate at the beginning of the lunch break. Bells sited at each of the gates (that by the main gate can be seen on the extreme left) were tolled at the beginning and end of each work session. Anyone reaching the yard after the bell had ceased would be marked as absent. As a result, these bells dictated the daily routine of a large proportion of the Chatham and Gillingham population, with this once popular ditty being sung in a number of the local pubs: There was a shipwright's daughter / Her name was Little Nell / And the only sound she ever heard / Was the sound of the dockyard bell.

THE ROYAL DOCKYARD at Chatham was one of the only major employers of women in the Medway area during the nineteenth and early-twentieth centuries. Working in both the ropery and colour loft, priority was given to those women whose husbands had died in naval or dockyard service. In this picture, drawn from a magazine published in May 1902, an artist has illustrated the duties of those women employed upon the manufacture of flags within the colour loft. The accompanying article explained that 22 women were employed in this task and the most 'capable' received 3s. to 3s. 6d. (15p to 17½p) per day. This amount, although having a much higher purchasing power than its equivalent today, fell far short of wages earned by skilled male artisans who were employed elsewhere in the dockyard.

MOVING BACKWARDS IN TIME, this picture illustrates Chatham dockyard's No. 2 dock as it appeared in 1858. At that time the dock had only just been re-opened following its rebuilding in stone. Prior to that date the No. 2 dock had been a much smaller timber dock. From the picture it is possible to get some idea of the purpose and nature of a dry dock. Fundamentally, they are large sunken ditches in which ships are built or repaired. The far end (or aft end) of this particular dock, behind which can be seen the River Medway, was sealed by a floating caisson. Once this was removed, water would flood into the dock allowing a vessel either to be floated in or out. Once the caisson had been returned to the entrance, the dock was pumped dry, allowing the workforce to get at the underside of the hull of any vessel that had been brought into the dock.

A FURTHER VIEW of the No. 2 dock. On this occasion the year in 1863 and the vessel inside is the future ironclad *Achilles*. Because docks were larger than building slips, it was sometimes necessary to construct the larger battleships within a dry dock.

ONCE A NEWLY BUILT SHIP had been launched (or floated out of dry dock) it was necessary to fit her out with the numerous additional items that made her a complete warship. In this picture of *Euryalus*, a steam frigate launched at Chatham in October 1853, shipwrights are busily engaged on the gun deck.

ONE IMPORTANT ITEM OF EQUIPMENT that was brought on board a warship during her fitting out phase was the guns. Here, during the early part of 1878, the frigate *Northampton* is taking on her battery of 18 ton muzzle loaders.

A CARTOON drawn by Jack Kettle in the 1950s illustrating the inevitable panic that occurred during the period when dockyard apprentices were undergoing exams.

THE DOCKYARD AT CHATHAM was closed in March 1984. During the period leading up to the final closure of the gates, this poignant message was chalked on to one of the walls of the sail and colour loft.

THE GROUP OF UNWILLING LABOURERS who undertook work on the huge extension that was constructed towards the end of the nineteenth century were convicts sent to Chatham as part of their punishment. To accommodate them, a civil works' prison was erected in the approximate area of the now abandoned naval barracks.

THESE CONVICTS were employed, for the most part, on the simpler tasks of digging out the basins and operating the brickworks. The more skilful were also employed upon construction work. In this illustration a number of convicts are seen undertaking masonry work on one of the four new dry docks that were part of the extension.

A FURTHER GROUP OF PRISONERS is seen here on St Mary's Island where they are employed breaking stones. These stones were later used in the walls of the new basin and dry docks. As many prisoners attempted to escape, the warders who guarded them were normally armed.

ANOTHER MAJOR BUILDING PROJECT that took place in the Medway area during the nineteenth century was the building of a waterworks at Luton. This photograph, which is of some of the arches designed to enclose the waterways, was taken in 1857 by an NCO instructor from the newly formed photographic department of the School of Military Engineering (now the RSME) Brompton Barracks. (RE Library.)

INSIDE THE LUTON WATERWORKS a Worthington Simpson beam engine was later installed for the purpose of powering the pumps. It was to remain in operation until the 1950s. (Southern Water Authority.)

THE GIANT WHEEL that was also part of the Worthington Simpson beam engine. During its operational life this regularly fascinated generations of local children. Often they would be seen peering into the pumphouse windows mesmerised by the constantly turning wheel and the endless gyrations of the beam.

View From Fort Pitt, Chatham.

A GENERAL VIEW OF THE RIVER MEDWAY seen from Fort Pitt and showing several centres of local employment. Along the right bank of the Medway the former Royal Marines barracks can be seen, along with the gun wharf and dockyard. The river itself provided additional employment.

WHILE TRAMS served the needs of those travelling within the towns, buses were essential for those who needed to travel further afield. In this view a Rainham-bound bus stands outside the George Inn at Newington.

EVENTUALLY the town trams were replaced by buses. Again, crewing these buses provided local employment. In this photograph a Chatham & District bus, bound for Gillingham, can be seen in London Road during the years immediately following the Second World War.

A FURTHER SOURCE OF EMPLOYMENT for those who lived in the towns of Chatham and Gillingham was farm labouring. In this photograph, a number of female hop-pickers are to be seen on one of the farms between Upper Luton and Hale. Unlike the mid-Kent farms, those in the Medway area rarely recruited their pickers from London, choosing to employ local residents on a casual basis.

ANOTHER GROUP OF HOP-PICKERS employed in the Luton area. Such work was undertaken during the month of September with payment always made on the last day of picking.

A GROUP OF LOCAL HOP-PULLERS. The task of the hop-puller was to pull down the hop bines so that they could be reached by the pickers.

A SCIENCE TEACHER is seen here in the chemistry laboratory of the County (now Robert Napier) School in Gillingham. The picture appears to have been taken during the 1930s.

GROVE ROAD SCHOOL, LUTON. Built in 1894 and enlarged in 1900, this school once provided facilities for 358 girls and 253 infants. In 1924 Miss Annie Emmett was the girls' mistress and Miss E. Burnet was in charge of the infants.

A GROUP OF PUPILS from Gillingham's Barnsole Road School. Dating to 1899 this school was constructed at a time when many new houses were being erected in Upper Gillingham. Following its enlargement in 1910 the school provided for a total of 1,398 pupils.

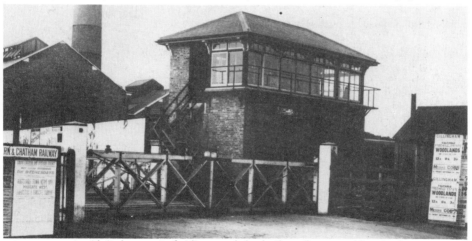

FOR GILLINGHAM, with its large set of sidings and sheds, the railway provides another source of employment. Visible in this picture is the signal box and crossing gates that adjoin Gillingham Road. Behind the signal box are the premises that once belonged to the Gillingham Borough Electric Light and Power Department (now SEEBOARD). Almost certainly this picture was taken before 1922, the year when the South Eastern and Chatham Railway ceased to exist.

The Windmill Darland Banks, Chatham,

A FURTHER GLIMPSE OF THE AREA'S RURAL PAST is provided by this view of the windmill that once stood on Darland Banks. It was demolished in 1924.

SECTION FIVE

At the End of the Day

The Strand – Gillingham Park – Victoria Gardens – Berengrave Lane – Luton – Chatham Tennis Club – Darland Banks – Zion Institute Football team – Gillingham Football Club – Luton Church Gymnastics Club – Chatham Empire – Theatre Royal – some Chatham and Gillingham pubs

Having considered some of the ways in which residents of Chatham and Gillingham were once employed, it is time to consider how this same community enjoyed itself at the end of the day. Not every means of entertainment has been included, with concentration mostly on early parks, some sporting activities and areas suitable for walking and riding.

The Strand.

The Incoming Tide at The Strand

JUST

Bandsta

THIS MULTI-VIEW CARD of the Gillingham Strand during the inter-war years gives some idea of the popularity of the area in these years. The circular bandstand (centre) and children's play area (top right) together with general landscaping were all added shortly before this series of photographs were taken.

The Strand.

Enjoying the Sun.
The Strand.

A SNAPSHOT VIEW of the Strand taken at around the same time as the previous multi-view card.

ANOTHER FEATURE of the Strand is an open-air swimming pool. Dating back to 1896, when it was little more than a depressed area of ground immediately above the high water mark, it has seen considerable alteration over the years. In this picture, dating from June 1920, the changing rooms seen along the side of the pool are actually converted railway carriages.

GILLINGHAM PARK. An alternative to the Strand, this park once offered twice weekly concerts. These were held in the (now demolished) bandstand that can just be seen immediately behind the railings on the right.

AMONG THOSE who might have performed in the Gillingham Park bandstand was the Gillingham Boys' Band seen here sometime before the First World War.

VICTORIA GARDENS, 1903. Situated in Chatham with a superb view of the River Medway, these gardens have frequently offered a few moments of solitude to those who have completed a busy day. First opened in 1897 to celebrate the Diamond Jubilee, the gardens were built on land once owned by the War Department.

VICTORIA GARDENS in 1933. A few changes have occurred in the intervening years. Most noticeable is the addition of a group of guns that have been placed under the flagpole. These had been captured during the Boer War and were subsequently presented to the town council.

FOR THOSE WHO WISHED TO TAKE ADVANTAGE OF THE COUNTRYSIDE there were once a number of excellent walks in the Rainham area. This is Berengrave Lane around 1920.

LUTON-CHATHAM—
The rides about here are
most enjoyable.

A PUBLISHED POSTCARD which celebrated the many country walks found in the Luton area. Despite the continued building of new houses, this card would not be totally inappropriate in the present day and age.

AN EARLY VIEW OF LUTON as seen from the top of Sugar Loaf Hill. The rural nature of the surrounding area can be fully appreciated. In the centre of the picture is Nelson Terrace (since replaced by Nelson Court) while Luton waterworks can be seen on the left. (Les Collins.)

A FAMILY GROUP enjoying the fine view that can still be appreciated from Darland Banks.

FOR THE MORE ENERGETIC there was the once decidedly middle-class sport of tennis. Here members of the Chatham Tennis Club, as seen during the early part of the present century, pose for an annual photograph. As a sign of the age in which the photograph was taken, one of the women on the middle row is wearing a monocle.

A SOMEWHAT LESS MIDDLE-CLASS SPORT was football. Members of the Zion Institute football team are seen here at the end of the 1911–12 season. (Mr N Burrows.)

FOR THOSE who enjoyed watching a good football match there were always the regular football matches played by Gillingham at the Priestfield stadium. This is a team photograph taken during the 1921–22 season. Along the top row, left to right, are the players: Sims, Marshal, Branfield, Waugh, Sissons and McAlpine. On the bottom row: McMillan (manager), Battiste, Freeman, Wood, Hall, Waterall, Kennedy (trainer). That particular season was not a happy one for Gillingham, the team finishing near the bottom of Division 3 (South). (Roger Triggs.)

THE GILLINGHAM TEAM for the 1925–6 season. In this photograph the back row is made up of, from left to right: Brown, Robertson, Ferguson, Butler. Front row: Edmead, Marshall, McKee, Rutherford (captain), the Mayor of Gillingham (Ald. J.J. Knight), Hall, Berry, Riddoch. Again, this was not a particularly outstanding season as the team finished in eleventh position. A further series of poor seasons were to follow with the team failing to be re-elected to Division 3 (South) in 1938. Eventually they were to return in 1950. For those who would like to see Gillingham reach the very pinnacle of success they might choose to read Neil Bell's novel, *My Brother Charles*. Set in Gillingham, it includes a chapter that sees the local football club fight its way through to the First Division. (Roger Triggs.)

THE LUTON CHURCH GYMNASTICS CLUB in 1946.

TWICE NIGHTLY AUDIENCES were attracted to the Empire in Chatham High Street where they were frequently entertained by the nation's top music-hall acts.

CURRENTLY UNDER THREAT OF DEMOLITION, the former Theatre Royal is seen here in its later career as a sports shop. First opened in 1899, the Theatre Royal was originally built for the purpose of showing popular plays performed by different touring companies. It was built at a cost of £30,000 and had the largest stage in Kent.

THE ALE HOUSE OR PUB has featured in the lives of Medway's population from time immemorial. As well as providing somewhere to relax at the end of a long working day, pubs also acted as the meeting place for local trade unions, friendly societies and political clubs. One such pub that was at the centre of eighteenth-century trade union activities at the dockyard was The Star on Chatham Hill. Although no longer in existence, the name of the Chatham Hill pub seems to have been transferred to The Star in Watling Street. This particular picture is of the later Star as it appeared in the 1920s. (Graham Smith.)

ONE OF THE OLDEST BUILDINGS in Gillingham is Ye Old Five Bells which is seen here sometime prior to the First World War. The building, which was built during the year 1700, has long served as a pub.

THE WHEATSHEAF which once stood in Claremont Place at its junction with Bryant Street.

THE LION, now the Green Lion, in Rainham High Street. (Graham Smith.)

AT THE REAL END OF THE DAY, time to return home. Housing land has always been at a premium in Medway, with this point clearly underlined by the closely packed houses to be seen in the area of Luton Arches.

A FURTHER VIEW of the packed working-class houses of Chatham and Gillingham can be seen in this early picture taken in Luton village. (Les Collins.)

CHATHAM.—As seen from a Handley Page Aeroplane.

ONE FINAL VIEW giving a further impression of the dense mass of housing to be found in the Medway area. A 1920s picture, it was taken from an early airliner which flew a regular route to Paris. This is one of several similar photographs which could be purchased by passengers as a momento of their journey.

Steamers Along the Medway

Queen of the South – City of Rochester – Medway Queen – Waverley – *motor boat to Upnor – the River Medway*

The Medway has long been a river that can boast a wide variety of shipping. Along its tidal reaches were once moored the mightiest warships of the Navy, while its creeks and bays harboured a veritable fleet of sailing barges and small fishing smacks. In more recent years, the river has seen the comings and goings of giant oil tankers, car ferries and a myriad of yachts and small leisure cruisers. Locally, one type of vessel has gained particular prominence within the common folk memory. This is the paddle-steamer, a vessel associated with day trips and holidays to the popular coastal resorts of Kent and Essex. For the most part, these steamers were owned by the Medway Steam Packet Company which later became the New Medway Steam Packet Company.

THE PADDLE-STEAMER *City of Rochester* outward bound for Sheerness, Clacton or Herne Bay. Built by J. Scott & Co. of Kinghorn (Fife) in 1904, she was the largest of the boats owned by the Medway Steam Packet Company. Powered by a 72 hp engine she was 160 ft in length. During the First World War the *City of Rochester* was acquired by the Admiralty and served as a naval tender at Chatham.

A FURTHER VIEW of the *City of Rochester*. Taken on 20 June 1908, she is on her way to Sun Pier where she will collect passengers going to Sheerness and Southend.

PURCHASED BY THE NEW MEDWAY STEAM PACKET COMPANY in 1924, the *Queen of the South* began life as the *Woolwich Belle*. Built in 1891 by Denny Brothers of Dumbarton, she had a relatively short period of service with the company as she was laid up in 1931.

THE PADDLE-STEAMER *Medway Queen*, outward bound from Strood, passes the Chatham and Gillingham shoreline. Another of the New Medway Steam Packet Company vessels, she was built at Troon in 1924 and was the first of the 'Queens' to enter service with the company. Taken over by the Admiralty during the war, she was one of the numerous small ships that were involved in the evacuation of Dunkirk. After the war she returned to the Medway before being laid up in 1963. At that time her future looked fairly bleak, but her rescue came in the form of her conversion into a club house moored in the River Medina on the Isle of Wight. A further threat to her survival occurred some years later when she was discarded in favour of a larger vessel.

IT WAS THE FEAR that this famous Medway vessel might be permanently lost, that led to the formation of a small company which was responsible for returning the ship to the Medway in 1984. Because of her dilapidated condition, she had to be mounted on a very inelegant pontoon. Here, the vessel is seen lying in Chatham Reach shortly after her return to the Medway towns.

THAT INITIAL BID to restore the *Medway Queen* folded through lack of money and eventually led to the creation of the 'Medway Queen Preservation Society'. In this picture the vessel, having now seen several more years of neglect, is taken from her dockyard moorings to Damhead Creek near Hoo where she is currently being restored. (Medway Queen Preservation Society.)

FOLLOWING HER WAR SERVICE at Dunkirk, when she made seven trips and saved over 7,000 lives, the *Medway Queen* was repaired and refitted at Chatham dockyard before undertaking minesweeping duties with the 10th Flotilla. This photograph, taken during her period as a minesweeper, shows members of her crew. For the most part, they were drawn from the naval barracks at Chatham. (Medway Queen Preservation Society.)

THE PADDLE-STEAMER *Waverley*. Although built in 1947 as a Clyde steamer the *Waverley* has, in more recent years, undertaken a number of annual cruises in the Medway. Here, the *Waverley* is seen leaving Gillingham for a cruise to Southend.

A MEMORABLE EVENT for some of the poorer children of the area was a boat trip to Upnor made in the summer of 1927. The children were drawn from the Medway Cottage Homes and Schools, these having originally been built by the local Poor Law Board for the purpose of accommodating children of those families living in the Chatham workhouse.

A FURTHER VIEW OF THE VISIT to Upnor made by children of the Medway Cottage Homes which were situated on elevated land close to Chatham's Maidstone Road.

THE START OF THE MEDWAY SAILING BARGE RACE of 1982 as seen from Gillingham Pier. At one time these Thames sailing barges would have been a normal sight for any of those passengers on board the frequent paddle-steamers that plied the local river. In earlier years the sailing barge was the veritable work horse of the river, used to carry such diverse loads as cement, farm manure and pots of jam.

A MORE GENERAL VIEW of the Medway looking towards Gillingham, as seen in the 1930s. Although taken on land, this picture gives an idea of at least one of the views that would have been gained by those on board a pre-war paddle-steamer.

SECTION SEVEN

A Naval Connection

Royal Dockyard – Navy days – ships' figureheads – HMS Pembroke – the Royal Naval Hospital

It was during the sixteenth century that the Royal Navy first started making use of the River Medway. Official records of the day indicate that it was during the year 1547 that local storehouses were first acquired by the Navy, indicating that thought was being given to something more permanent than the possible arrival and departure of the occasional warship. Over the years, this naval presence considerably expanded, with the entire fleet ordered to the Medway in 1550. Subsequent years saw the establishment of the dockyard, followed by a victualling yard and gun wharf. Between them, these institutions were responsible for the construction, repair, provisioning and arming of a large proportion of the Royal Navy's warships. In time, the area lost some of its earlier importance, with Portsmouth re-emerging as the main centre of naval activity. Chatham and Gillingham continued to play an important part in servicing the needs of the Navy, a point underlined by the opening of the naval barracks (HMS Pembroke) and hospital at the beginning of the present century.

CHATHAM DOCKYARD seen from the Upnor side of the river during the year 1902. A number of warships are to be seen in the nearest, or No. 1, basin while, on the horizon to the extreme right, Jezreel's tower can just be seen through the mist.

AT CHATHAM DOCKYARD the 10,600-ton battleship *Camperdown* seen sometime around the year 1902. Built at Portsmouth, *Camperdown* was probably brought to Chatham for a period of dry docking prior to her returning to the fleet.

A SERIES OF PHOTOGRAPHS showing the launch of the newly built armoured cruiser *Shannon* on 20 September 1906. Following her launch she was to be taken round to one of the basins for fitting out.

Navy Week, Chatham.   *Model of County Class H.M.S. Kent from*

DURING THE INTER-WAR YEARS, the dockyard began a tradition of throwing its gates open to the public for Navy Week (later Navy Days). One of the early attractions was this motorized model of the Chatham-built cruiser, *Kent*. The real *Kent* was launched in 1926 and was the largest cruiser to be built in the yard.

THE LEANDER CLASS FRIGATE *AURORA* decked out for visitors to the 1976 open days at Chatham dockyard. *Aurora* had just completed a major conversion at the dockyard, having been modernized for a primary anti-submarine role.

VISITORS going on board *Aurora*.

ONE OF THE MAJOR ATTRACTIONS at the 1981 Chatham Navy Days was the Type 42 destroyer, *Coventry*.

SUBSEQUENTLY the 1981 Chatham Navy Days proved to be the last of these extremely popular events held at the dockyard. The planned 1982 Navy Days were cancelled as a result of the Falklands crisis. A regular attender at all of the later Navy Days were the three Chatham-based ships of the Inshore Survey Squadron, *Egeria, Enterprise* and *Echo*.

ONCE A FAMILIAR SIGHT at Navy Days and on the Medway off Chatham and Gillingham was the Royal Naval Auxiliary-operated *Loyal Helper*.

CIVILIAN STAFF belonging to the Royal Naval Store Depot seen here during the inter-war years.

THE 'COUNTY' CLASS GUIDED MISSILE DESTROYER *HAMPSHIRE* is towed through the Bull's Nose entrance to Chatham's No. 3 basin on 3 June 1976. She had been brought to Chatham for disposal, parts of the ship being cannibalized for other 'County' class destroyers then in commission. (M.o.D.)

AT ONE TIME Chatham dockyard had its own official museum which displayed various items connected with ships that had either been built or based at Chatham. This photograph was taken around the year 1902 and shows some of the figureheads which were once housed in this museum.

PRIOR TO THE CLOSURE OF THE DOCKYARD in 1984 a number of ships' figureheads were positioned either side of the Admiral's Walk that led down to Queens Stairs. This particular figurehead belongs to *Terpsichore*, a wooden corvette that was launched on the Thames in 1847 and was subsequently brought to Chatham where she was sunk following torpedo trials in October 1865. The figurehead was detached from the vessel after she had been raised for breaking up.

THE FIGUREHEAD FROM THE *BRITOMART* SLOOP which also stood on Admiral's Walk. Despite the information on the plaque, it seems likely that this figurehead came from the *Britomart* that was launched in 1847 and subsequently broken up at Chatham in 1874.

THE SUBMARINES L.11 and L.25 at Chatham during the 1920s.

A STEAM CRANE that once stood off Chatham gun wharf, probably photographed during the 1880s.

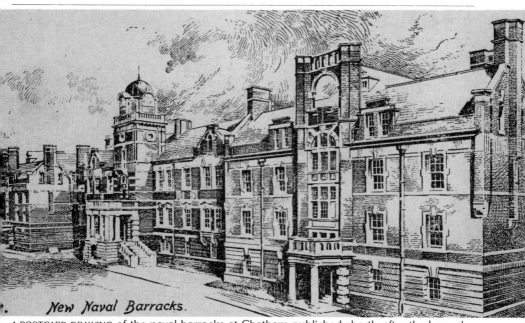

New Naval Barracks.

A POSTCARD DRAWING of the naval barracks at Chatham published shortly after the barracks were opened in April 1903. In order to build the barracks, the Admiralty had acquired the site previously occupied by Chatham Prison. Work on the new barracks began in May 1897. The official opening of the barracks was considered by many as an anti-climax to an important local event, for it consisted of nothing more than a formal 'march in' of the 5,000 officers and men who initially occupied the various accommodation blocks.

ROYAL NAVAL BARRACKS, CHATHAM. 319.

AN EARLY PHOTOGRAPH of the main building to the naval barracks. Completed by December 1902 it was designed by Sir Henry Pilkington.

A GENERAL VIEW of the accommodation hulks that pre-dated the Pembroke naval barracks.

R.N. BARRACKS, CHATHAM.

THE ENTRANCE TO THE BARRACKS from the adjoining dockyard. Most of those based at the Chatham naval barracks would serve on board ships that were maintained and refitted at the dockyard.

NAVAL RATINGS taking rum into the naval barracks for subsequent distribution as part of the traditional naval rum ration.

THE NEW NAVAL BARRACKS was a marked improvement over the earlier hulks and included, in addition to the accommodation blocks, numerous facilities for the recreation, exercise and education of both officers and seamen. This photograph shows the petty officers' canteen.

DISTRIBUTION OF THE 'GROG' or rum ration at the naval barracks. Rum was first introduced into the Royal Navy following the conquest of Jamaica in 1687. By the date of this photograph the daily grog ration to ratings consisted of one and a half gills of water to half a gill of rum. The ration was discontinued in 1970.

THE MEN'S READING ROOM at the naval barracks as seen before the First World War.

CHATHAM NAVAL BARRACKS, the mess room in the officers' quarters.

THE NAVAL BARRACKS BOWLING ALLEY.

ENTRANCE TO THE COOKERY SCHOOL. Among tasks undertaken at Chatham naval barracks was the training of ships' cooks. The railway line was part of an internal system used for bringing supplies and other stores to the nearby victualling depot.

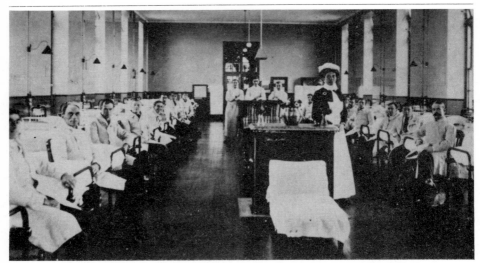

KING EDWARD VII officially opened a new naval hospital in Gillingham in July 1905. Replacing a much smaller hospital that stood opposite the main gate to Chatham dockyard, the new hospital was equipped for 500 patients. Today, the building still remains. No longer a naval hospital, it has been renamed Medway Hospital and serves the local community. It is possible that this picture was taken shortly after the outbreak of the First World War.

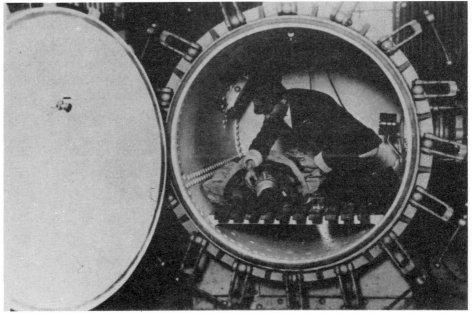

SOMETHING OF A MYSTERY PICTURE HERE. Possibly something to do with one of the Navy open days, it appears to show a diver receiving the attentions of a naval officer.

SECTION EIGHT

The King's Shilling

The Lines – Gillingham Fort – Brompton Barracks – Edward VII's visit to Gillingham – RE Balloon Section – St Mary's Barracks – Fort Pitt

As well as a considerable naval connection, the towns of Chatham and Gillingham also have a long association with the army. For the most part, this stems back to the beginnings of the dockyard and the need to provide a landward defence for this important national arsenal. Of particular importance was the construction of the Chatham and Gillingham Lines during the eighteenth century. This necessitated a considerable increase in the numbers of troops posted to the Medway towns and eventually led to the construction of St Mary's barracks and Brompton barracks.

TROOPS posted to the Chatham and Gillingham Lines were never called upon to fire in anger. Instead, the nineteenth century saw a number of military manoeuvres carried out on the Lines. These usually consisted of one regiment or collection of regiments attempting to gain possession of the Lines while another regiment acted in its defence. A very popular spectacle in its day, thousands descended upon the Medway towns in order to view the day's events. In this engraving from an 1861 edition of the *Illustrated London News* troops are seen at the advance with a band providing appropriate music.

PRE-DATING THE LINES was the fort at Gillingham. Constructed as a direct result of the Dutch raid of 1667, the fort once stood on St Mary's Island. Designed for 'fifty peeces of canon' it slowly fell into ruin and would have been quite unable to repel an enemy within only a few years of its completion.

R.E. Barracks and Band, Chatham

THE ROYAL ENGINEERS AT BROMPTON BARRACKS have a particularly close affinity with the towns of Chatham and Gillingham. In fact, members of the Corps have been posted to Gillingham since 1807. This Edwardian postcard shows the RE Band performing before members of the public who, it must be supposed, had entered the barracks as part of some open day.

KING EDWARD VII visited the barracks at Brompton on 26 July 1905 for the purpose of unveiling a memorial to those corps members who had been killed during the Boer (or South African) War of 1899–1902. After carrying out this ceremony the King proceeded to the new naval hospital in Gillingham where he also officiated in the opening ceremony of this building. In this contemporary postcard view, King Edward VII is to be seen more or less in the exact centre, partly obscured by the detached stone plinth.

EILING THE R.E. SOUTH AFRICAN MEMORIA

S. A. War Memorial, R.E. Barracks, Gilling

ANOTHER MEMORIAL to be found in Gillingham barracks is this arch dedicated to those who fell in the Crimean War. The adjacent statue, which is of a Boer soldier, was another memorial to the South African War. In later years it was sent by the Corps to South Africa.

AN EARLY VIEW of the memorial to General Gordon within the precincts of Brompton Barracks.

PHOTOGRAPHED around the year 1914, members of the Corps are seen erecting a suspension bridge. The building behind (now the Royal Engineers museum) was the electrical school which had been constructed during the years 1902–1907.

A VIEW OF THE BROMPTON BARRACKS PARADE GROUND as seen during the inter-war years.

MEMBERS OF THE RE BALLOON SECTION, 1888. The balloon section, which was based at St Mary's Barracks, was responsible for developing the gas balloon as an observation platform. Those to be seen on the back row (from left to right) are: sappers Sykes, G. Allen, J. Allen, Price and Lance Corporal Champton. On the bottom row are: sappers Greener, Fitzpatrick and McEwan, Sergeant Smith, Lieutenant C.P. Close, Major Watson, Lieutenant H.B. Jones, Corporal Bryant and sappers Wookey, Wiffen and Walker. The RE Balloon section was actually under the command of Colonel J.L.B. Templer who was also appointed superintendent of a balloon factory actually established at St Mary's Barracks.

SAPPERS from the locally based Royal Engineers at work in an open-air cookhouse.

AT THE TIME OF THE CRIMEAN WAR a number of wounded soldiers were sent to St Mary's Barracks to convalesce. This engraving appeared in the 21 July 1855 edition of the *Illustrated London News* and is of a group of invalided soldiers at Brompton who had been paraded during a visit by Queen Victoria.

ANOTHER OF THE WOUNDED seen by Queen Victoria at the time of her 1855 visit to St Mary's Barracks, was Corporal Courtenay of the 44th Regiment. His injuries were received during an attack upon Russian rifle pits before Sebastopol, when Courtenay was hit by seven bullets. It should be noted that St Mary's Barracks, which stood on land adjacent to the Royal Naval barracks, were demolished in the 1960s.

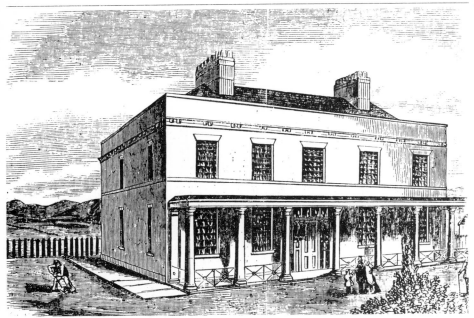

THROUGHOUT PART OF THE NINETEENTH CENTURY the hospital at Fort Pitt also received soldiers who were considered insane. The building seen in this engraving was constructed for their accommodation, although in later years the insane were despatched to Fort Clarence in Rochester.

ONE OF THE MOST IMPORTANT MILITARY HOSPITALS in the area was Fort Pitt. Originally built to help defend the dockyard, it was being used as a hospital throughout much of the nineteenth century. Although difficult to verify, it seems likely that this picture was taken in the grounds of Fort Pitt and shows both the nurses and the wounded who were at the hospital during the First World War.

SECTION NINE

A Moment in Time

Hen and Chickens, Luton – The Mulberry Tree – Gillingham Civic Centre – Lower Rainham Road – Brompton Barracks – The Siege of Symons Avenue – the future King George V at Chatham – Military Pageants – VE Day Parties – An Air Display – HMS Endurance – Alexandra Flag Day – Medway Institute – Luton Road – Fort Amherst – Gillingham Fête – Farewells and Funerals – Scouts and Guides

This final section is a fairly general look at particular moments captured by the artist or photographer. Ranging from an idyllic view of nineteenth-century Gillingham through to various twentieth-century pageants and parties, other moments in time are the events surrounding the siege of Symons Avenue and the return of Endurance from the Falklands.

MIDDAY AT THE HEN AND CHICKENS in Luton. Photographed before the age of the tram, a few local workmen and a disconsolate ice-cream salesman pose for the photographer. The deserted horse bus, belonging to H. & J. Kent, has just completed the normally profitable journey from Strood that would have taken it through Chatham High Street.

A GROUP OF 'REGULARS' outside the former Mulberry Tree pub in the Lower Rainham Road. This photograph seems to have been taken around the year 1905.

ANOTHER PHOTOGRAPH taken in Lower Rainham Road is of this group of houses situated between Bloors Lane and Pump Road.

LONDON ROAD. Once little more than a quiet country lane it has, with the arrival of the motor car, developed into an extremely busy (and often hazardous) thoroughfare used by thousands of vehicles every day of the week.

GILLINGHAM CIVIC CENTRE shortly after its opening in September 1937.

BROMPTON BARRACKS, 15 January 1916. The aftermath of a serious fire which destroyed the whole of the barrack block in the North Square. The fire, which started in the fodder store, had been discovered at 8 p.m. the previous evening but was not brought under control for several hours. To help fight the blaze, the army had to call for the assistance of both the Gillingham fire brigade and the Chatham Volunteer Brigade. Although the nation was in the midst of a major war, sabotage was not considered a possible cause.

THE SIEGE OF SYMONS AVENUE, Chatham, Wednesday 6 June 1951. Senior police officers try to get some idea of progress in a massive police operation to stop a crazed gunman from firing indiscriminately into the surrounding street. The gunman, Alan Derek Poole, had previously shot and killed a Chatham policeman, PC Alan Baxter. (Kent County Constabulary.)

AFTER POOLE HAD SHOT PC BAXTER on the Monday of that week, he successfully eluded a massive police search but was eventually discovered over a day later hiding out in his parents' house in Symons Avenue. The siege began around 8 o'clock on the morning of 6 June 1951 when Poole had opened fire upon police officers keeping watch on the house. Neighbours were quickly evacuated and the Army was asked to provide support. Over the next two hours a barrage of shots was exchanged, with a police marksman eventually killing Derek Poole. (Kent County Constabulary.)

A SENIOR DETECTIVE is seen holding the gun that Poole used both to murder PC Baxter and during the siege of Symons Avenue. It was a lethal weapon, a Sten gun that Poole had previously stolen at the time of his desertion from the Army. The full story of the siege can be found in *Murder in Kent* by Philip MacDougall. (Kent County Constabulary.)

A PHOTOGRAPH that first appeared in the 31 January 1936 edition of the *Chatham Observer*. Published shortly after the death of King George V, it shows a youthful Prince George (who was not to become George V for a good many years) during the period 1877–1892 when he served in the Royal Navy. In fact, he is seen at Chatham while serving on board the first class gunboat HMS *Thrush*. This ship was his first commission in the Navy. The future King George V is standing in the centre of the group behind Queen Alexandra. On the right of Queen Alexandra is Admiral Sir Henry Keppel while King Edward VII is standing on the extreme left of the picture. Also to be seen in the picture are Queen Maud of Norway (seated on the right of the picture) and Princess Victoria (seated on the left of the picture).

HAILED as 'the finest spectacular display which residents of these towns have had', September 1913 saw naval ratings from HMS Pembroke barracks enact a fictional scene from the Boxer uprising of 1900. Somewhere in the region of 400 sailors participated in the display that ended with an attack on a Boxer-held fort. This photograph, showing an early scene from the production, is a view of the parade ground which had been turned into a market place imagined to be somewhere on the Chinese coast.

A NUMBER OF SEAMEN WERE KIDNAPPED and taken to a fort at one side of the parade ground as the play developed. This fort was later placed under siege, presenting the public with an impressive finale to the day's event.

APART FROM THE PLAY based on the Boxer uprising, visitors to HMS Pembroke on that occasion were also invited to witness electrical, wireless and diving displays, while in one of the sheds a Blériot aeroplane was on display. A particularly popular event was this field gun display.

ANOTHER SCENE from the field gun display at the Chatham naval barracks.

THE CHATHAM DIVISION OF THE ROYAL MARINES, whose barracks were once located in Dock Road, also held an annual display that was open to the public. For their open day held in August 1912 the theme was a history of the British armed forces from the time of the Romans. In all, 197 officers and men were involved together with a further 50 who represented the modern day army and navy. In this picture a group of Marines represent the Royal Navy at the time of the Battle of Trafalgar. In the centre of the picture one of the Marines represents Admiral Horatio Nelson. Some local residents had been highly amused by this particular group as, earlier in the week, they had been involved in selling programmes in the High Street. During a sudden downpour, Admiral Nelson had been forced to take shelter under the entrance dome to the Empire theatre!

PERHAPS THE LEAST FORTUNATE OF THE MARINES involved in their 1912 pageant was the man delegated to dress as Queen Boudicca. Doubtless, over the following weeks, he had to overcome a great deal of ribbing from his fellow comrades.

ANOTHER SCENE FROM THE ROYAL MARINE PAGEANT of 1912 was a group dressed as Roundheads and Cavaliers from the Civil War period.

A VE DAY PARTY held on land at the top of Chatham Hill. The picture shows a number of residents from the area. The land on which the party was held was owned by Mr Hook, a horse breaker. Mrs Hook can be seen to the right of the picture.

VE DAY PARTIES were held throughout the Medway towns to celebrate the end of the war in Europe, with this mammoth party held in Gillingham's Victoria Street. Notice the general absence of young men. They, of course, were still on the continent of Europe or involved in the continuing hostilities with Japan.

WITH THE DOCKYARD LESS THAN TWO YEARS FROM FINAL CLOSURE, during the Summer of 1982, HMS *Endurance* returns to the dockyard after a period of service in the South Atlantic. Because of her involvement in that year's Falklands crisis, she was welcomed by thousands of local residents who lined the Gillingham river bank.

AS PART OF RAF WEEK held at Chatham in May 1981, the Red Arrows provided a breath-taking air display over the River Medway. This photograph shows them flying just beyond the tower of the former parish church in Chatham (now the Heritage Centre).

VOLUNTEERS who were involved in the collecting of money during a pre-First World War Alexandra flag day. At the appropriate time of year, these distinctively dressed women would be seen throughout the streets of Chatham and Gillingham. Much of this money was for St Bartholomew's hospital, a charity hospital that could only have survived on the goodwill of those who annually donated their time, money and support.

AS PART OF THE BREAK UP of the poor law institutions, the Chatham Cottage Homes Schools (set up by the Board of Guardians) were handed over to the adjoining Rochester Council in 1927. Renamed the Balfour Road Schools, it meant that children of the schools could now compete with all other children living in the area.

NAVAL CADETS parade along Luton Road. Although the date is unknown, it must be around the time of the First World War. (Les Collins.)

THE GILLINGHAM CARNIVAL of 1982 included this re-enactment of the Napoleonic Wars.

FRENCH NAPOLEONIC SOLDIERS at rest during one of the first 'living history' displays held at Fort Amherst.

SCENE OF A FAREWELL DINNER held in the grounds of the White Swan Inn at Chatham on Monday 30 January 1854. Those attending the dinner were helping Admiral Sir James Stirling celebrate his coming departure to take command of the East India and China Fleet.

THE FUNERAL OF GEORGE NEVES, former editor of the *Chatham News*. George Neves was one half of the Parrett and Neves partnership that had been responsible for purchasing the *Chatham News* in 1885. The declared aim of the newspaper at that time was to provide 'copious, accurate and impartial reports of all meetings, whether Conservative or Liberal'. George Neves died and was buried at Sittingbourne during the 1920s.

ANOTHER FUNERAL OF LOCAL IMPORTANCE was that of Admiral Corry, held at Chatham on 29 January 1907. Corry was Admiral Superintendent of the dockyard at the time of his death. The funeral cortège attracted huge crowds.

A TOTAL of 8000 guides came to Gillingham Park in June 1926 where they were inspected by Princess Mary (daughter of King George V). Members of the public were admitted to the park by ticket only, but the price did include tea. According to one local newspaper, 'the spectacle was a unique and most impressive one, the sun shining on the rather sombre hue of the girl's uniforms brought out the colour until the whole resembled a field of bright blue corn flowers . . . ' The photograph reproduced above shows a local group of guides led by Miss Collins. Gillingham Park bandstand can be seen on the left. Miss Collins undertook the role of camp adviser during the arrangements for the royal visit.

PREPARATION FOR THE ST GEORGE'S DAY PARADE held at Chatham on 20 April 1913. Here, scouts are drawn up by the side of the Town Hall, with the district scout master, A.J. Tassell, preparing to inspect them. After this photograph was taken, the scouts marched to St Mary's Church where the sermon, preached by the Revd E. Godfrey, included an appeal for St Bartholomew's hospital.

ACKNOWLEDGEMENTS

I would like to thank the following people who kindly loaned me photographs from their private collections to appear in this book: Les Collins, Graham Smith, Mr C. Taylor and Roger Triggs. In addition, the Corps of Royal Engineers Library (Brompton Barracks), Marks & Spencer plc and the Southern Water Authority were also kind enough to allow me to use a number of their photographs.

Special thanks must also be reserved for the staff of the local libraries who patiently answered a number of questions and searched through their various files in order to discover small pieces of historical information.

Finally, I would like to mention Mrs Noreen Chambers of the Medway Queen Preservation Society. Not only did she supply information on the *Medway Queen* but also searched out a number of interesting photographs. For those interested in joining the Medway Queen Preservation Society, can I suggest that they write to the Society at 81 Park Avenue, Gillingham.